A JOURNEY TO REMEMBER: POEMS

A JOURNEY TO REMEMBER: POEMS

Jai Narayan

To order additional copies of this book, contact:
Xlibris Corporation
1-888-795-4274
www.Xlibris.com
Orders@Xlibris.com
34295

CONTENTS

To
My parents, who are
no more,
and
My wife and children
with love

There was a roaring in the wind all night;
The rain came heavily and fell in floods;
But now the sun is rising calm and bright;
The birds are singing in the distant woods.
　　　　　　　　—William Wordsworth

A JOURNEY TO REMEMBER: POEMS

This collection of poetry, blank verses, expresses the author's unique experiences and imagination. A reader will experience numerous moods and facets of love in the poems. The author also examines the intricacies of life and pain caused by the evil acts of man. He shows his great admiration and appreciation for the beauty of the natural world.

In the "Mount St. Helens," he admires the creation and beauty of nature:

> It stood for years with its majestic beauty,
> With perennial snowcapped peak,
> A tourist wonder of the Golden West,
> Along the picturesque coast of the Pacific!

Certainly, this collection of poetry is a moving journal, written with smooth language, of thoughts and feelings of the author.

ACKNOWLEDGMENTS

I would like to express my sincere thanks to Xlibris Corporation for publishing my poems. My gratitude is also to everyone at Xlibris who has helped with the publication of this book. Finally, my love and thanks to my daughters, Seema and Reema, who have read the manuscript and typed it for submission.

WANDERER

Slowly the clouds drifted away
The Eastern sky became clear
The Hunter of the East
Was seen journeying Westward
The sentiment of glee was in the air
There was neither sound nor noise
But in the woods far . . . away
The nightingales were singing
In the bewilderment of the endless joy.
The wanderer paused and listened
To the song of the happy season
He could neither tell nor guess
Whether the songs were of some pain
Or they were just songs—in loneliness
The wanderer said, "Whatever they sang
Was blissful in the season."
Suddenly he saw the Hunter had reached
The journey's end
And it painted the West
With golden and crimson red
The West wind then
Whispered in the wanderer's ears,
"Hurry home! Hurry home! Hurry . . .
Before the evening shadow devours thee."

GRAND CANYON

Thou art a super creation
Of a timeless work of a river,
Zigzagging in downward quest,
Tortuously eroded thee,
Into a most intricate works of art!
As a Nature's living wonder,
With unmatched grandeur on earth,
Basking in peace and solitude.
The river with its copious waters
Roars dangerously between thy walls,
Boisterously on downward journey.
Thou art a Nature's mystic canyon,
Once I stood on thy rim
And my legs trembled with fear!
Yet I managed to see thy charm
In the vastness of thy silence.
The river's eternal works of art,
How magnificent is thy name:
Grand Canyon of the Golden West!

SPRING

There's no season like Spring,
So showy and beautiful!
Flowers bloom and grass spring,
Happiness and joy are in plentiful,
While the birds twitter and bees buzz.
Winds blow with sweet fragrance
In the cloudless, breezy days,
And the peacocks, in the park, dance!

THE POPPIES
(CALIFORNIAN POPPIES)

The beautiful golden poppies
Of the slopes, hills, and vales,
Looked so sensuous and vibrant,
In the breezy Spring's sun
Of the Golden West.
I stared at their elegance
On the rolling hills of the West.
Thousands at a glance, saw I
In their exuberant mood.
They bloomed beyond the hills,
Fluttering in the gentle breeze:
Like the ripples of the waves,
I was moved by their sight;
And was lost in their world.
As I bent irresistibly to touch
The poppies in their joyful motion,
Then I heard a voice from the hills:
"Keep away from the golden poppies,
The pride and flower of the State,
Of the Golden State of the West!"

MOUNT ST. HELENS

It stood for years with its majestic beauty,
With perennial snowcapped peak,
A tourist wonder of the Golden West,
Along the picturesque coast of the Pacific!
And within the Mount was a sleeping giant,
A dormant, fierce, and killer volcano,
Which in the early Summer of the eighties
Erupted and blew the top of the Mount.
The force of the explosion measured
As the power of several megaton atom bomb.
And the pyroclastic flow from the eruption
Devastated miles and miles of vegetation,
Sadly two hundred thirty square miles in all.
The tall trees fell and lay dead as matchsticks.
A lake, streams, and rivers choked with debris;
And the lush forests disappeared from the scene.
The monstrous blast killed scores of people;
And the volcanologist David A. Johnston
Died gallantly while reporting from the region.
And the hero's body was never found,
But his last historic words on the air,
Still echoes in the eternal silence,
At the base of the mighty Mount St. Helens:
"Vancouver, Vancouver . . . This is it!"

ICEBERGS

The scorching Summer's heat
Drove me out of the house.
I sought shelter under the breezy
Tall and shady coastal pine,
Near my neighbor's wooden fence.
As I stood cooling my burning soul,
I saw pretty blooming roses;
In my neighbor's garden,
Of varying sizes and colors,
All swaying in the gentle breeze.
But the giant white roses
Outdid the others in the breeze.
And I asked the dancing white,
"What name shall I give thee?
Oh sensuous beauty of the season!
Thou art prettier than the snow
In the bitter Winter of the North."
Then a voice from the garden came:
"They're already named—Icebergs."

THE MOUNT EVEREST

Towering in the infinite sky,
Is the world's highest peak,
In the Himalayan Range,
The reverend Mount Everest:
Asia's natural glory!
Far below this planetary peak
Are countless gushing springs,
Numerous roaring cataracts
And perennial rivers, too.
All issuing from the Himalayan
The eternal snowcapped Range.
The holy rivers: Ganges and Jamuna,
Indus and Brahmaputra
All rushing down to merge
Into the calm Indian Ocean.
And the mighty Everest in the Range
Stands majestically—watching,
High above the milky clouds.
For centuries, it lured the daring climbers
To its timeless charm!
Many died in their quest to conquer,
But some made it to the top.
Now, the Asia's royal pride, the Everest,
Branded as a Mount without mercy;
But the magnificent Everest
Gazes at the world below,
As if from another planet!

A FESTIVE SEASON

The Northern Sun wasn't hot,
But there was dampness in the air.
Many trees were turning gray, brown,
Yellow, orange, and it was a sign of Autumn.
Thus the trees were getting ready
For a bitter and unkind Winter!
Some trees had already shed their leaves;
And the branches looked sad and naked.
The snow on the mountain peaks
Hailed the coming of—White Christmas,
And a welcome sign of a festive season!

THE MORNING BREEZE

The early morning breeze
Was gentle, brisk, and cool.
The flowers seemed dancing in the breeze,
And the breeze in its gleeful mood,
Swayed the Jasmine shrubbery.
The countless innocent petals
Fell to their untimely demise.
The cruel breeze swept the petals
Far, far away—from the grieving shrubbery!

THE HAYMAKER

The blistering heat of the Summer sun,
Transformed the picturesque hills,
Vales and plains into dull lifeless color,
Of endless gray and brown.
As I walked down the rolling hills
Which gently merged into a vast plain,
There I saw an old haymaker,
Busy cutting his ripened hay.
Unaware of the scorching heat,
He seemed to be in a joyful mood,
Singing and resting as he worked,
His strenuous task until dusk.

SOME SLEEPLESS NIGHTS

Some sleepless nights
Would scare the life to death;
And the life would go on
Without the precious sleep.
The sleepy eyes would crave
For a peaceful night's sleep.
The poor mouth would yawn
For a good night's sleep,
But the helpless mouth
Would remain wide open
For hours in the darkness.
The tired body would lie
Lifeless like a dead log,
In the stillness of the night.
The mind would wander
In the world of nightmare.
The intellect would freeze
And refuse to function,
In the sleepless nights.

OCEAN

Ocean, thou art ugly
And a restless fool.
A demon without a form,
I've watched thee rise
And fall without pain.
Thou art never at peace,
You swell and foam
Like a hungry dragon.
Fed by streams and rivers,
Glaciers and rain alike;
But I've never seen thee
Flooding like streams and rivers,
I think and wonder why?

A MAJESTIC SPECTACLE OF CHRISTMAS

The long-awaited season, bleak Winter,
Came at last with abundant powdery snow.
The snow-laden trees shivered in white Winter
And the drooping branches moaned with heavy snow.
Oh, the Nature was in fury with piercing cold!
The chilling blizzards were frequent on the plains
And the bleak Winter was icy cold.
Yet the season's white silvery beauty on the plains
Became a majestic spectacle of Christmas,
Amidst the crinkling joys and jingling bells of Xmas!

FLOOD

The evening was calm.
The birds in the woods
Were unusually cheerful.
Amidst their retiring noise
I fell asleep at dusk.
At midnight, I was disturbed
By a sudden scary noise.
There was thunder and lightning;
The weather was terribly unruly.
The howling wind was frightening!
When I peeked through a window,
I saw the streetlights were out.
The night was horribly dark;
But I could hear the pouring rain.
The nearby stream roared;
Seemed it overflowed its banks.
Sound of the rushing waters could be heard!
And as I groped in the darkness,
I heard someone screamed, "Flood!"

PARTING

"Ah! What a painful
Experience is parting,"
Said a parting leaf
To a mourning tree.
"I was stuck to you
For how long . . .
My memory fails to tell,
Every moment was treasured.
Our anger and bitterness
Were all consumed
By our closeness.
But now as I part,
In tears and sadness,
My heart breaks in pieces!
Soon I'll be blown away,
Far, far away . . .
To a place unknown,
By the wind so unkind!"

After hearing the leaf,
The tree cried in silence,
And murmured in tears:
"Sad is the parting,
But there's an end
To all existing things.
The God has made
No exception in his creation.
The parting is inevitable,
Therefore, may you have
A pleasant journey!
And somewhere rest in peace,
May heaven's blessing
Shower upon you."

MORNING DEW

Like countless diamond
I saw at a glance,
Hanging on the grass,
Glittering like the stars
In the early hours of the morn.
I walked gently on the grass,
To feel their short existence.
My gentle and soft walk
Made them to disappear;
Seemed without any pain,
Sadly leaving behind
A watery track to wonder!

THE TWIN TOWERS

The unshakable Towers stood firm
Like the ageless rocks of Gibraltar,
Against fierce winds and storms
For three scores or more years!
Once the terrorists' coward acts
Failed to bring the Towers down.
On 9-11, unaware of the disaster,
In thousands, workers rushed to the Towers,
As usual, to resume their work.
Amidst the day's busy activities,
Some workers heard the sound of explosion.
Oh! Terrorists' hijack airplanes
Penetrated the Towers with mighty force,
Like several megaton bombs.
The explosions set the Towers on fire;
Terror and confusion were everywhere.
Many helpless workers jumped
From the fiercely burning Towers,
Oblivious of the deadly consequences.
They dropped like toys from the sky
To their untimely death!
Many heroes: police and firemen
Rushed to save the workers
From the burning Towering inferno.
In their heroic mission to rescue,
The rescuers got trapped;
And many died in the mighty mission!
At last the burning Towers crumbled!

The New Yorkers were stunned and shocked,
To see their great historic pride:
The Towers in ruin beyond imagination!
Perhaps, in an hour the Towers
Became a huge mass of twisted steel,
Pieces of concrete, glass, and dust.
Three thousand or more perished
When the Towers unmercifully collapsed.
Eighty Nations or more mourned for years
For they lost their priceless assets:
The workingmen and women!
People still mourn for their loved ones
With sad memories in their aching hearts!

OH, WATER!

Oh, water! thou neither have a form
Nor color, a shape, or texture,
Yet a vital essence of life.
A sustainer of all existence,
And clear as crystal in thy appearance.
Once I saw a child at play,
Terribly curious in thy world,
Repeatedly kicking and grabbing
In a tub full of thee.
But thy kept escaping the child's grip,
Making the child furiously angry.
At last the child gave up and screamed,
In the presence of the mother's eyes;
Who smiled and lifted the child
From a tub full of thee.
Oh, thou art so cunning
And armed with magical skills.
I may well call thee a wizard,
In thy monstrous force and flow,
Nothing can escape from thy ravaging path.
Yet thou art so indispensable,
And inseparable from our existence.
Oh, water, thou art the most glorious one!

THIS CHRISTMAS

The season's crisp and bitter winter wind
Brought unimaginable powdery snow.
Unmercifully the snow covered
The hills, mounts, and valleys!
The snow-laden shrubbery and trees
Stand motionless—in the exhilarating
Christmas season of this year!

DISASTER IN THE PARK

A monstrous killer slab
Of old granite rock,
In the Yosemite National Park,
Disintegrated in fury
From the high face of a cliff.
It thundered with a cloud of dust,
As it made its way downward,
And struck the Happy Isles.
Many visitors and hikers
Ran frantically for their safety.
A hiker was crushed to death!
The sky above the Happy Isles
Was covered by the dusty cloud.
The Nature was out of control,
And the broken rocks
Swiftly moved downward.
They uprooted countless trees
And left a snack shop in shambles!
An area over fifty acres
Was left in a sad state,
As a living monument of Nature's
Awesome power of destruction!

I'M TOO TIRED

I'm too tired!
I worked hard
For seven scores,
During Summer and Spring,
Autumn and Winter alike.
I raised a family
And contributed my share
To humanity at large.
Now my limbs ache
Both night and day.
I can hardly carry
My own burden
And hate to be a burden.
Now my pain and sufferings
Are my private affairs.
My only wish in life
Is to lie down quietly,
In some empty space
Without thinking of pain,
Like a fallen leaf
In a white winter.

LOST LOVE

When I looked back with tearful eyes,
I saw my love had gone far away!
Far beyond the reach of my watery eyes,
And I could only hear her cry from far away.
As I cried, warm tears flooded my eyes,
And drop by drop it eased my pain away.
Once again like a lion I cried with my watery eyes,
And pleaded her not to run away.
Ah! I longed to embrace her with my watery eyes,
Like the ocean embraces the wild waves.

UNTIMELY BURIAL

In the holy month of Ramadan,
A day became sad and gloomy.
The heaven suddenly obscured,
But the angels watched,
And cried in silence!
Their tears fell as light rain;
Amidst such pain and sorrow,
We buried our friend's
Beloved wife to rest in peace!

EXPLOSION IN THE SKY

The ill-fated flight 800,
With a jubilant group of people,
Was on a Paris-bound flight!
The Boeing flew on its normal route,
At dusk from a noted coast.
Everything seemed well with the flight;
The veteran captain ordered calmly
To increase the flight's altitude.
These were his last recorded words
In the orange box—often called as black.
Then there was a sudden bang;
The plane exploded like a bomb.
People momentarily saw the sky on fire,
Burning bits and pieces of the plane
Fell forcefully in the ocean.
The powerful jet fuel
Set the ocean on fire.
It burnt for long hours
And made the rescue impossible.
By the daybreak not a survivor found!
All feared dead and sunk in the ocean.
The news of the horrible tragedy
Flashed across the world.

The world was stunned,
But the gallant rescue went on
Tirelessly for weeks—day and night.
Bits and pieces of bodies were picked,
And people prayed with reverence for days.
On the sand and beaches of the ocean
They even dropped flowers and wreaths,
In the waters of the Atlantic, too.
The Nation mourned the loss for days,
And is still mourning
The most unforgettable tragedy . . .
Of the sky near her historic coast.

THE FOREST

I stood in utter shock
Where once a forest thrived.
Now the ground is naked,
Sadly, as bare as a desert.
Once for miles the giant trees
Were monarchs of the region.
Who knows, for how long,
Perhaps for centuries and more.
Now the forest had gone,
The undergrowth disappeared, too.
All forms of forest lives
Were mercilessly destroyed.
Many fled to some strange places,
When their home, the forest gone.
Once the birds sang here;
They twittered and flew freely.
Crickets and insects chirped;
Butterflies fluttered in multicolors.
The honeybees buzzed on flowers;
The monkeys joyfully played,
On the forest's high canopy.
The forest's beauty and life
Were exuberantly beyond record.
But, now the forest gone,
Its music and songs are dead.
The unkind destroyers of the forest
Were the loggers saws and axes.

THE HOUSE ON A CLIFF

The house on a cliff
Perched like an eagle's nest.
It was a sight of beauty,
Of a joy and envy too.
Down below the cliff
The ocean raged and roared.
The giant breakers rose;
Dashed their heads against the cliff.
Unaware, the house stood firm
On the solid ageless cliff.
But on a calm Summer's day,
The Nature's uncontrollable force,
Shook the rocks beneath the house.
The cliff cracked and trembled!
And the house lost its grip;
It crumbled with the cliff,
And fell into the ocean below;
Devoured by the angry waves.

PILGRIM'S MESSAGE

The pilgrim was old indeed,
Bent with drooping head,
Carried the years' burden
On his aging and aching back.
He resembled as an old pine,
On a deserted cliff by the ocean,
Bent and battered by harsh wind.
But the pilgrim looked strong,
As he marched on a pilgrimage.
He prayed reverently at dusk
And marched on his sacred journey.
Each dawn brought him a new hope
And closer to his heart the holy place.
When he reached a village in the desert,
He went to the village's common well,
To quench his days-long thirst.
Moved by the old man's state,
A civil village boy at the well,
Gracefully gave the man water to drink.
And after a pause the boy asked:
"Oh, dear traveler, where thou headed,
In this unkind weather in the desert
Torturing thy weak and weary soul?"

The old and compassionate man,
With a heavenly smile of joy he replied:
"Oh, you kind young soul,
I'm on my way to the holy place,
Where our beloved prophet
Preached the message of brotherhood,
And stressed—there's only one God"
Thus the old man replied,
And marched on in the direction
Of the Black Stone—the Kaaba.

THE POND

The heaven was clear and calm,
Not even a patch of cloud was in view.
The wind ceased and refused to blow,
The pond looked quiet and gracious!
There wasn't even a ripple
On its placid surface,
Which glittered and glowed
In the blistering heat of the sun.
I was moved by the pond's silent grace!
Now after many decades,
In my utter loneliness,
I still see the lonely pond,
So tranquil in the cosmic space,
Of my imagination—still glittering!

THE UGLY FOG

The Sun disappeared below the horizon
Like a huge ball of fire,
Only the crimson glow was in view.
Then came the uninvited fog;
It fogged the glow as it moved.
Enraged the sunset viewers by the Bay.
The city and the bridges of the Bay
Were engulfed by the ugly fog.
It drifted like a Chinese dragon,
And made the monotonous foghorn to blow.
The irritated viewers had nothing to view,
Cursing and frowning at the ugly fog,
The viewers returned to their fog covered homes.

IN THE STORMY NIGHT

The tempest raged and ravaged,
As a phantom of the darkness.
The wailing wind was appalling,
I looked through a peeking hole;
And saw the sky totally obscured.
The heaven roared and thundered!
The rain poured with a maddening force.
I stood with fear by a flickering lamp,
With its dying dimmed yellow rays.
I heard a man moaning in the storm,
Somewhere near my lonely hut.
With compassion, I left the door ajar,
For the man outside in the dreadful night!
I waited for him for hours with my sleepy eyes,
But no one came in the stormy night.
I fell asleep beside my flickering lamp,
And entered into a world of dreams!

WHAT WE LEAVE BEHIND

We came with nothing
In this rugged world.
The life from the beginning
To the end is a struggle.
It's like an empty journey
In this world of false realities.
We claim nothing in it
Nor do we take anything from it.
When we exit this crazy world,
We only leave some tiny specks
Of some good deeds done,
On the long rugged journey
As our priceless marks.

MY BLACK BEAUTY

She was a petite,
Her skin was glossy
From head to toe.
Her big round eyes
Glowed mischievously,
When I saw her
In a garden party.
Her attire was least
In the Summer's heat.
She tiptoed nonstop
During the party.
My searching eyes
Followed her steps
In absolute obscurity.
By midnight I was drunk
And I lost the sight
Of my black beauty!

DEATH

Oh, cruel death I saw thee
At a very close range!
The heart which was full of life,
It lost its rhythm with the age.
The lungs made the chest
Rise and fall as the low tide,
At the twilight of his life.
His mouth gently opened
For the last drops of water,
As it touched his withered lips,
The soul struggled in vain,
To utter some words of farewell,
But the lips couldn't say a word.
The eyes which glittered once,
Were dimmed and dismal;
And stared at the empty space above.
Then the head gently tilted;
And the eyelids dropped.
The fragile body seemed relaxed
With the final breath of life,
The soul then peacefully departed!

LOVERS' PLEA

Oh, you beautiful night
You have just begun,
How infinitely tranquil thou art
So tender in the early hours.
Pretty Queen of the night,
The moon is up in the heaven.
A glowing inspiration for lovers,
And has been for ages!
What a night, the glittering stars
Gazing at us as we stand.
Our warm lips and hearts
Have just barely touched;
Pleading in silence,
Oh, night, stay a little longer!
Don't hasten your journey,
Or else our tender hearts
Will break like sand castles,
On a beach by cruel waves!

THE INNER LIGHT

I rambled alone
From one block to another.
I often got lost
And tired as I walked.
I was utterly confused;
And cursed the world
For no reason at all.
My long walk seemed endless;
And I reached a dead end.
I stood there bewildered;
And I closed my eyes.
I found peace all around me;
And saw—The Inner Light:
The Self-Divine!

CHILDREN ON THE SHORE

When the tide had gone
Far away from the shore,
I saw hundreds of children
Playing with sand in the sun.
They created tiny worlds of their own:
Sand castles, forts, mounts, and hills,
Under the watchful eyes of the parents.
The children screamed and ran;
They jumped and bathed in the sand;
Laughed and cried as they played.
Their noise mingled with the breeze
And it echoed as sweet melodies,
Which still I bore in my heart!

IF I HAD WINGS

If I had wings like a falcon,
And mighty speed and power of a twister,
Then I would soar over the clouds
And carry you to the Moon.
Undisturbed we would sail
To the Queen of the night.
Far, far away from the murky
And polluted-troubled earth,
And far away from the foes,
The polluters of the earth.

I'M DIVINE

I'm as precious as a gem,
I'm the infinite space,
From the very beginning,
I'm in thee concealed.
Thou art unaware of my being,
I'm in thee and thou art in me.
Thus we coexist
From the beginning,
I'm thy breath and life,
And center of all existence.
In this infinite space,
I'm the essence of manifestation,
Of all perfection.
Therefore, indisputably
My being and I'm Divine!

THE MOON

Oh, you luminous beauty,
The solitary creature,
The Queen of the night,
How often I wondered
About your true existence:
Cheese, icicle, a dewdrop
Or a piece of diamond . . .
Gliding alone in the space so high,
Illuminating the darkened world
As you softly go by.
But, at last the mighty man
Had revealed thy secrets.
You're nothing but an ageless planet,
Covered with white powered rocks
With no form of life at all.
Yet, so sublime and gracious,
The world will love and sing:
The song of your eternal luminary,
As you travel in the boundless space,
As long as the Sun and Stars exist!

A REDWOOD

I stood at thy massive base
Like a frightened midget.
Thou looked so gigantic
With thy scary towering stem,
Yet, I call thee a tree.
A marvelous creation of God,
Made thee in the name of a tree.
The king of the trees in the wild
As a living monument
Of some unknown past.
Standing like a slumbering giant
With a green towering crown,
Above the floating milky clouds.
And how oft man has praised
Thy glorious past and majestic heritage,
Still towering in the forests of the West.

THE TWISTER

I stood in utter bewilderment,
To see my years life's possession
Scattered in pieces beyond recognition,
By a twister so violent!
It devastated the entire village
Where mostly the seniors,
Retired and poor lived.
Some even died in the twister's path.
I wanted to scream and cry,
But my voice choked.
My emotion and tears froze,
Then I said to myself, "I must cry."
At last I leaned . . .
Against a twisted pole,
And watched the people in pain!
I started crying and tears poured,
To watch my village in ruin,
By a violent twister so unkind!

BLACK MAN'S DREAM

For decades the black man's fate
Was in the white man's hand.
The black man lived in terror,
With an uncertain future.
Often the white man's whip,
Unmercifully fell on his back.
And the master amused himself
In his cruel and inhuman act,
In this promised land of the West,
Which has no relics of feudalism;
But, it has a cruel history of slavery.
With changing time and the laws,
The cruel system of slavery,
Came to an end in the land of the free.
The black man was made to believe:
"All men are created equal."
For decades the black man fooled himself;
And painfully he learned,
There is nothing equal,
In the white-dominated domain,
Where wealth and power reign.
And black man's problems still exist,
And his dream of equality
Is just another story of his dream.

WE DIFFER

You and I differ:
You're like a drifting log,
Lost in the wild currents
Of the fast and turbulent life.
But I float like an iceberg,
Hidden in the depth
Of the ocean of wisdom.
You see life as a vision
In its empty present state.
But I contemplate and worship,
And go beyond its existence and core,
Try to understand, what is it?

THE DESERTED LANE

I looked down the deserted lane,
My memories like a lightning flashed back.
Then I remembered my childhood past,
In the lane, where I spent my early days
With friends and neighbors' kids.
The lane would burst with life,
With our noise, laughter, and play.
At times we fought and cried,
But, when tomorrow came, the yesterday
Was forgotten with smiles and cheer.
That was the beauty of the kids in the lane,
Now, the lane is quiet and deserted.
The children grew and gone!
Many old neighbors have died;
Some painfully retired in solitude.
Now, only silence reigns the lane,
And wherever I looked in sadness,
I felt the presence of a glorious past
And the memories echoed into my ears!

A FLYING SPIRIT

A flying spirit
Said to a worried king:
    "I'm the monarch
    Of the boundless space,
    I fly East and West,
    North and South freely.
    I've neither foe
    Nor boundary to cross.
    I eat and sleep
    Where my journey ends.
    But you move with fear
    With uneasy crown
    Within your kingdom's borders.
    You live in fear
    In your limited world,
    But I see the world
    In my free self."
Thus the flying spirit spoke
And soar into the endless sky,
Leaving behind the king to wonder!

THE BERTHA'S FRENZY

Bertha, a fierce tropical hurricane
Raged from the Caribbean Sea,
Violently changed its course.
It roared with varying velocity;
Energized by the warm Gulf waters.
Thus the Bertha pushed on and on,
Unmercifully like a hungry dragon,
Along the North Carolina coast
And far beyond as the Hugo did.
Pounded and battered the Myrtle Beach;
Tourists deserted their favorite resort.
The coast residents were ordered
To run inland for their safety,
From the uncontrollable force of the Bertha.
It uprooted trees and flooded
The roads and knocked the power lines.
It blew the roofs of the buildings,
The debris flew like papers
By the stormy wind in the heavy rain.
Thus, the Bertha in its fury, left behind
A hideous and unimaginable ruin,
Along the Eastern coast of the South.

THE PORCELAIN BEAUTY

Oh, you porcelain beauty,
The prettiest thing of creation,
The creator's masterpiece,
A marvelous work of art!
I admire thee in solitude
And praise thy creator,
Who created thee as a wonder!
A woman, yet like an angel
With unchangeable beauty,
As firm as a marble statue
And smoother than a mannequin.
Yet thou art prettier
Than a polished mannequin,
With or without attire.
What shall I call thee?
A timeless treasure!

MY WEDDING

In the early hours
Of my wedding day,
Half awake and half asleep,
I had a dream:
Heavenly maidens and angels
Came into my room,
Singing and dancing with joy.
They whispered into my ears:
"Oh, you angel of angels,
Today is your wedding;
Two hearts will be united
In eternal matrimony."
Thus they said and gone.
Left me alone
In my wandering thoughts.
Now as I sit and wonder,
In this joyous mood,
I say to myself:
"The glitter and the splendor
Of this great hall tonight
Will not be here tomorrow.
You all will be gone
Like the maidens and angels,
But, I'll be left alone
With the fondest and the sweetest
Memories of you all!"

LIFE'S THREAD

A spider built his cobweb
On a branch of a tree.
A gusty wind blew the cobweb;
The spider fell from his web.
Hanging by his life's thread,
He leaped upward with a force
Toward his ruined cobweb,
But he failed as he tried.
The scary spider looked downward;
He saw a hungry reptile watching.
When he turned his head upward,
He saw a writhing tree snake
On the branch of his cobweb.
Thus the life of the spider
Was hanging dangerously,
Between the two demons
By a thin life's thread.
The spider knew the death
At any moment, was inevitable.
So, with all his courage he hanged on
And waited for the moment,
To say farewell to the cruel world.

THE DUST STORMS

Beneath the rainless sky of the plains,
The vast rich farm country
Transformed into an endless waste.
Once the great pride of the farmers,
Now it lay dead as a lifeless desert.
Farmers prayed and stared at the sky,
But not a patch of cloud was in view.
The plains baked in the scorching sun;
And it cried silently during the day,
In the intolerable heat of the sun.
When the pressure dropped,
The wind blew violently in the plains;
It lifted the plowed rich soil
Miles high and moved as a monster.
The frequent dust storms dimmed the sun,
And devastated everything in its ugly path.
Thus the year's severe drought
Gave rise to killer dust storms,
Which left the plains in utter ruin!
"Oh, God alone knows," said an old man,
"When the life will be normal
In our Great Beloved Plains!"

THE OLD OAK

The old oak is still standing
Near the old farmyard.
Some buildings have collapsed;
Others have gone forever.
The old good farmer
Had died decades ago.
The stone on which he sat
Under the oak, on a hot day,
Is still there, eternally settled.
Though the farm had been deserted,
But the aging oak still grows stronger
And reminiscing the glorious past.

THE DEVIL'S SLIDE

A magnificent cliff
Facing the mighty ocean
Like an antique beacon,
Hundreds of feet high
Above the Pacific Ocean.
The huge breakers rise
And fall dashingly
Along thy picturesque coast,
Day in and day out.
Thus the roaring waves
Pay their homage to thee.
The famous fog of the coast
Kiss thy face as it rises
Above thy stately head.
For decades we watched
Thy existence in amazement.
There's nothing devilish
About thee above the ocean.
Thy charm and fascination
Brought the cliff lovers
To thy feet for years.
Though you slide off and on,
In small chunks and bits,
That's a Nature's awesome course
And beyond thy control.
Therefore, there's nothing
So devilish about thee.

I WANT TO KISS

I want to kiss you, is my wish.
I have known you for so long,
There's nothing more, now I wish.
I'm just longing for a kiss!
I feel like embracing you
And take you far away
Like a violent storm.
Thus my passion rages for you,
Yet, I try to calm myself.
Still my angry passion rises
And falls like wild waves
On a rough and stormy day.
Ah, what a passion for just a kiss,
Please, for a kiss sake, let me kiss!
Once, once only for my heart's sake,
The aching heart for your kiss!

IN SOLITUDE

How long was I in solitude?
I don't remember now,
But the mystical experience
And the bliss of the eternal peace,
Ventured me into the unknown,
To experience the unknowable
In the vastness of the space,
Beyond my earthly existence.
Thus my solitude became
A blissful condition of union,
With the mystical peace within
In the infinite silence of the universe!

THE BEAUTY OF LIFE

The beauty lies hidden within,
Buried behind the walls
Of the poor caged soul.
There alone it glitters and glows,
That's the pure beauty of life.
And it only emanates itself
When the soul bursts with joy;
And the eyes sparkle like diamonds,
Tears trickle down the cheeks,
Then the world shares that joy.
That's the real beauty of life
Which each soul longs from life.

WHEN YOU'RE ALONE

When you're alone,
Far and far away . . .
See and remember nothing,
Except a lonely cloud
Drifting by on a clear day.
Then pause and think back
And listen to the passing wind.
What music it sings to the ears?
Perhaps of some sweet bygone days,
Murmuring in silence as it passes by.

THE BEACH BY THE CLIFF HOUSE

The swirling fog came and engulfed the beach,
And the glimmering sand below the cliff house.
I sat by the window and watched the thick milky fog.
Saddened by the ugly change in the weather,
I madly sipped wine glass after glass.
The mood of the people in the house
Changed with the unpleasant weather.
Then the fog gently retreated like a bride's veil;
By noon the sun burst out of the cloud.
The ocean looked wild and restless
Like a hungry serpent in the wilderness.
The insane waves rose and rolled;
They madly banged and dashed with foam,
On the beach by the cliff house.
People cheerfully ran on the beach
To hear the sound of the wild ocean,
And to watch the sand and pebbles
Which waves flung back and forth on the beach.
I stared at the beach and people for hours;
And then I left the cliff house with joyful feeling,
Before the evening fog engulfed the beach again!

WHERE I WAS BORN

In a small farm village
Perched in a river valley
On a sugarcane farm,
Amidst the valley's greenery,
So I was told.

The house was small,
A simple island cottage
With grass-thatched roof
And dry bamboo walls,
So I was told.

There was neither clinic
Nor a hospital around,
So, I was delivered at home
By a village midwife.
So I was told.

I was an unusual urchin
Of the peaceful village.
Some called me a devil
And many hated my gut.
So I was told.

At two I set a house
On fire and pushed a girl
In the village well.
I was a little terror.
So I was told.

At six I entered
The village school.
By fourteen I was well
Disciplined and groomed.
So I was told.

THE FAITHFUL ROOSTER

The faithful rooster
Was the village pride.
His punctual crow
In the morning hours
Was the village alarm.
The farmers rushed
To their village farms.
The women into the kitchens
To cook the morning meals.
The faithful rooster
Never missed a crow.
He made his home on a mango tree
By the common village well.
One cold morning
The rooster didn't crow.
A woman went to the well
To get a pail of water,
She saw the rooster lying
Dead under the mango tree.
She told a neighbor
About the rooster's death,
The sad news spread
From mouth to mouth
Like a lightning in the sky.
At midday the villagers
Gathered in sadness,
To bury the faithful rooster
Under the mango tree!

MY FATHER

My Father, neither could he write
Nor could he read a word,
Literally he was illiterate.
But, he was a learned man!
He carried in his small head
Years of valuable wisdom,
Which couldn't be found in books.
His sharp vision and experience
Were his best teachers.
We acknowledged with reverence
His wisdom and knowledge.
He had left us some years ago;
We missed him sadly each day.
But, still we feel his presence,
And find comfort in his divine thoughts,
A priceless legacy he had left behind!

A MAIDEN'S WISH

The Moon was full in the heaven,
Shining in the cloudless space.
I gazed at her absolute calmness,
For hours in the moonlit night.
Her magic inspired poets for ages,
And made the lovers to fall in love.
With these wandering thoughts of the Moon,
I moved on in the moonlit night,
I saw a pretty maiden on the meadow,
Leisurely walking and lost in her thoughts.
I paused and wondered at her sight:
I asked, "What could've brought her here,
Alone, on the meadow far away from home?
So late at night in the silence of heaven."
She gracefully looked at the Moon;
Then she knelt in prayer on the meadow.
I wondered what she could've asked,
In her prayer from the Queen of the night,
Then I remembered—a maiden's wish,
Like in the prayers on the Saint Agnes' Eve,
When young, pure, and pious maidens pray,
For a vision of their loves delight.
The solitary maiden on the meadow that night,
Couldn't have wished anything more,
Than what her heart desired in solitude,
The blessings of an eternal company in her prayers!

OUR PRIDE AND JOY

I didn't have a verse or song
To welcome thy happy birth,
But the heaven rejoiced with light rain.
On a religious day before thy birth,
We prayed to the Goddess of light.
And our prayers were answered:
With thy birth as a symbol of wealth.
A nurse herald with joy—"A girl!
Oh God, now even the heaven rejoices
In the early hours of the morn,
With the blessings of Indra—light showers,"
And hours later thy parents named thee:
Nikisha NARAYAN, the Godly name.
Thy glittering eyes and sweet smiles,
Both bring endless joy to our hearts,
Thou'rt our family's first pride and joy.

LOVE—BIRDS

Two birds with silvery wings
Clung to a branch of a tree.
They stared at each other
With wondering and loving look;
As their friends watched them
With a surprise and gracious wonder!
One moved closer and closer
And fondly embraced the other.
Then he whispered softly:
"Let's march together,
On this long journey of life!"
The other confirmed
With twinkling eyes.

MOTHER'S DEATH

Mother's long journey of life
Very gallantly came to an end.
She died peacefully at home
In the early hours of the morning,
Perhaps just around the prayer time.
She could have died while praying,
In the holiest time of the year.
But, outside the Nature was in fury,
Clouds burst and rain poured,
In the night and all day long,
Amidst rain and storm, the next day
We took our beloved mother
On her final long journey,
To a sacred resting place
And as we arrived . . .
We saw the sky become darker;
The dark rainy clouds stood still.
The unruly Nature became calm
And finally the rain stopped.
Ah! What else one could have wished.
We all prayed with heavy hearts,
Fondly in sadness and with tears,
We buried our beloved mother.
In the hillside graveyard,
Near others to rest in peace!

PRIMROSES

Brilliant, jubilant, and vibrant primroses
Thousands at a glance saw I,
Gently fluttering in the breezy Spring.
They were under the spreading canopy
Of a giant oak near a historic castle.
And many beneath the thick foliage,
Of green shrubbery along a fence.
They were sparkling and peeking
In many shades: red, pink, yellow, white, and purple.
Incredibly they were the pride of Spring!
But around them the blue Forget-me-not
And the red fiery Bleeding Hearts,
Insanely they stole my heart away.
And yet at a second glance saw I,
A host of Japanese Primroses—Japonica,
In brilliant shades of red and white
Around the stems of White Emperor Tulips.
And the English Primroses in radiant blooms,
Underneath the tall stems of Daffodils,
All whispering their joys in the season,
And secretly they won my heart in loneliness!

THE SEASON'S CYCLE

At last the long bitter Winter was gone;
The snow in the valley started melting.
It flooded the streams and the brooks,
And they roared down to the ocean.
Then the long-awaited Spring arrived;
The lifeless trees without leaves came to life.
The grass grew and the flowers bloomed;
The bees buzzed and the butterflies flew.
The valley once again was full of life,
Ah, but the Spring's stay was short.
The Summer with its scorching heat
Came too soon to slay the heavenly Spring.
Once again the ground became dry;
The vegetation parched in the Summer's heat.
The streams and the brooks dried again.
The beasts were running wild for water;
Many died as they panted for breath.
But, man alone, somehow survived
From the Nature's torture and pain.
The season's cycle continued and ended;
With the breezy Autumn and the blue sky.
Then once again the season's cycle began,
With the bleak Winter and its chilling wind and snow.

THE SPIRIT OF CHRISTMAS

The hasty Spring made way
For the long blistering Summer.
But the brief cool Autumn
Sadly herald the coming
Of chilling snowy Winter.
Once again with its Splendor
Came the spirit of Christmas!

THE TULIPS

Shall I compare thee to a Spring's day,
Nay, thou art more gentle and pleasant
Than the rhythmic smiles of Spring,
Yet, I compare thee in false pretense!

Oh! the swift wind of April
Shakes the blooming buds of Spring,
Petals fall with breaking hearts,
Mourn! for the parting memories of the past,
But you bloom as if to eternity
And unaware of the fleeting time!

If the unkind time devours thee
And thou'rt gone, but to return,
Presumptuously to the season's call,
Till then said I unto thee, "Farewell
And glitter in my eternal lines!"

THE FROSTY CHRISTMAS

The bitter frost is everywhere:
On the grass, trees, and windowpanes.
The trees are gray and leafless,
But the icicles on the branches
Hang and glitter in the morning sun.
Crispy, brown, and gray leaves
Lay lifeless on the frosty ground.
The hills and mounts are covered with snow
And the frosty Christmas is everywhere!